# a to Z

Christmas

Beverley Mathias
and
Ruth Thomson

Illustrations: Emma Iliffe

Watts Books
London/New York/Sydney

Watts Books
96 Leonard Street
London EC2A 4RH

Franklin Watts Australia
14 Mars Road
Lane Cove
N.S.W. 2066

© 1990 Franklin Watts
This edition. 1995

ISBN: 0 7496 0363 1

Editor: Ruth Thomson
Series Design: Edward Kinsey
Design: Sarah Crouch

Illustrations: © Stephen and
Emma Iliffe

Photographs: courtesy of British
Turkey Information Service T;
Camera Press portrait study by Karsh
of Ottawa Q; J Allen Cash
Photolibrary L; Chris Fairclough A, B,
C, D, G, I, J, K, M, O, P, R, S, U, X, Y,
Z, Christingle; ZEFA cover, E, F, H, N,
V, W.

Typesetting: Lineage, Watford

Printed in Italy
by G. Canale & C. S.p.A. - Turin

About this book

* This book has been designed for use by all people learning to read. It is both an information book and a reading book.

* The alphabet is used to provide a natural framework for the exploration of the book's topic and for language development.

* The simple sentences place the key words in context and extend appreciation of the subject.

* The superb photographs have been carefully selected to stimulate interest and discussion.

* The activities that conclude the book are designed to reinforce understanding and to encourage further involvement in the topic.

* A special feature of the book is the provision of Signed English and the Finger Spelling Alphabet for non-hearing readers. This feature is also intended to provide a fascinating introduction to sign language for all readers, teachers and parents.

Beverley Mathias
Ruth Thomson

Aa

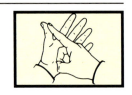

This is an **advent** calendar.

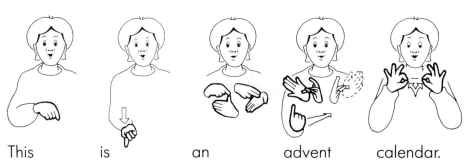

| This | is | an | advent | calendar. |

Bb

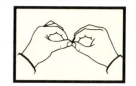

Shiny **balls** hang on our tree.

| Shiny | balls | hang | on | our | tree. |

Cc

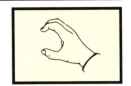

Crackers go bang!

Crackers   go   bang!

Dd

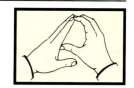

Decorations are fun to make.

Decorations   are   fun   to   make.

Ee

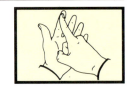

Some **evergreens** flower at Christmas.

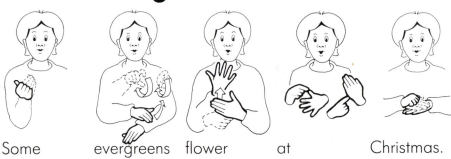

Some   evergreens   flower   at   Christmas.

Ff

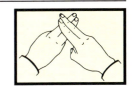

Father Christmas gives out presents.

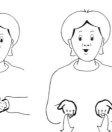

Father   Christmas   gives   out   presents.

Gg

These **garlands** are brightly coloured.

| These | garlands | are | brightly | coloured. |

Hh

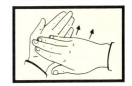

Holly **has red berries at Christmas.**

Holly   has   red   berries   at   Christmas.

Ii

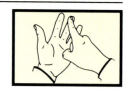

Our cake has white icing.

Our   cake   has   white   icing.

Jj

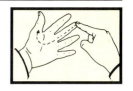

Jesus was born on Christmas day.

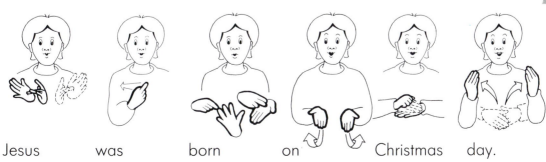

| Jesus | was | born | on | Christmas | day. |

Kk

Three **kings** journeyed to see Jesus.

Three   kings   journeyed   to   see   Jesus.

Ll

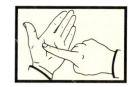

The tree glows with **lights.**

| The | tree | glows | with | lights. |

Mm

Mince pies are tasty Christmas food.

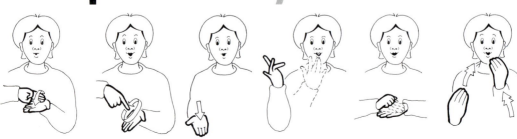

| Mince | pies | are | tasty | Christmas | food. |

Nn

Here is a **nativity** scene.

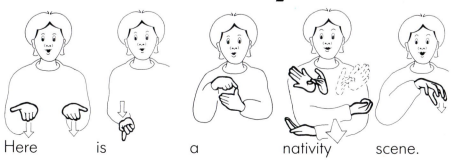

Here   is   a   nativity   scene.

 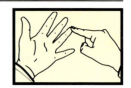

There are **oranges** in this stocking.

| There | are | oranges | in | this | stocking. |

Pp

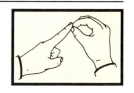

I wonder what these **presents** are?

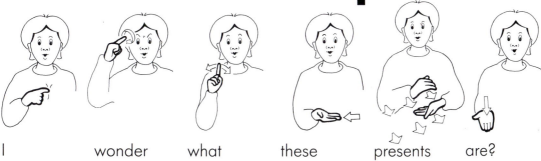

| I | wonder | what | these | presents | are? |

Qq

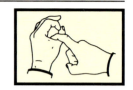

The Queen speaks at Christmas.

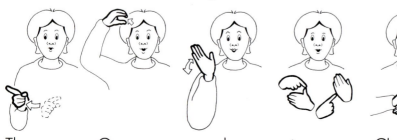

The   Queen   speaks   at   Christmas.

Rr

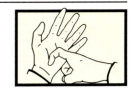

This card has a fat robin.

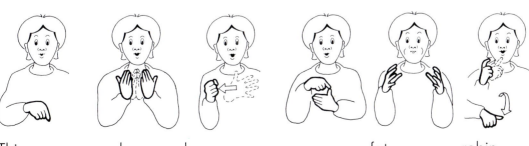

This   card   has   a   fat   robin.

Ss

The shepherds came to see Jesus.

The   shepherds   came   to   see   Jesus.

Tt

People eat roast **turkey** for Christmas.

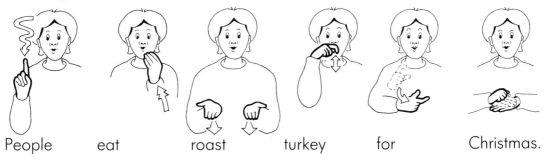

People   eat   roast   turkey   for   Christmas.

Uu

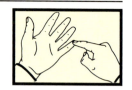

All our presents are unwrapped.

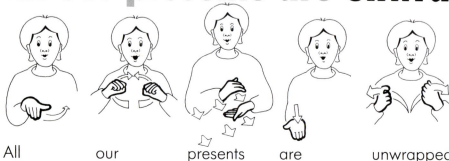

| All | our | presents | are | unwrapped. |

Vv

Our **voices** fill the air.

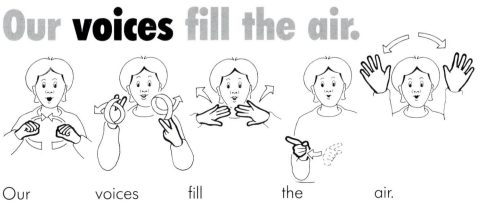

Our   voices   fill   the   air.

Ww

People hang wreaths on their doors.

| People | hang | wreaths | on | their | doors. |

X x

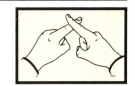

Christmas is really exciting.

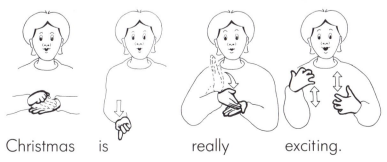

Christmas   is   really   exciting.

Yy

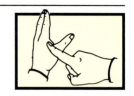

Chocolate **yule** log is delicious.

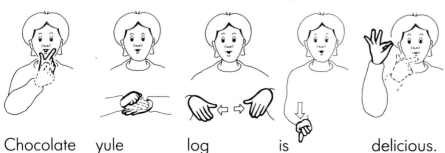

Chocolate   yule   log   is   delicious.

Zz

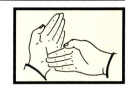

Grandpa sleeps after dinner. Zzzzz.

Grandpa   sleeps   after   dinner.   Zzzzz.

Tissue snowflakes

Make some tissue snowflakes in different colours to stick on to your windows at Christmas time.

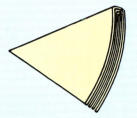

3 Fold the semi-circle into thirds to make a triangular shape.

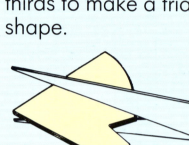

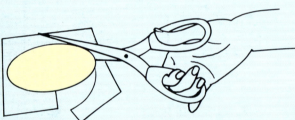

1 Draw round the rim of a mug or a cup on to tissue paper. Cut the circle out.

4 Snip shapes on all three sides with a pair of sharp scissors.

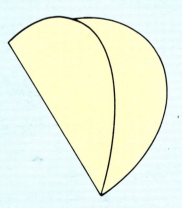

2 Fold the circle in half.

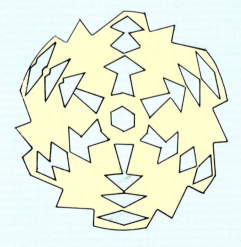

5 Unfold the paper to look at your snowflake.

Christingles*

Christingles are made for a special children's service held just before Christmas in some Christian churches. The orange represents the world and the light represents Jesus, the Light of the World, who was born at Christmas. The four sticks are the four seasons of the year and the ribbon is the girdle of God's love around the world. Make a Christingle of your own.

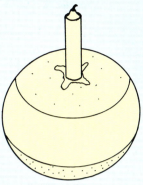

3 Push the candle into the cross in the orange. Spread the corners of the foil over the orange.

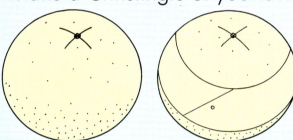

1 Cut a cross in the top of an orange with a sharp knife. Cut a piece of red ribbon long enough to fit around the middle of the orange and fasten it with a pin.

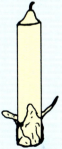

2 Cut a 2cm square of foil. Wrap it carefully around the base of a small, white, household candle.

4 Find some peanuts in their shells, raisins, small squares of cheese, glacé cherries and four cocktail sticks. Put three of the foods on to each stick and then push the sticks into the orange so that they form a square.

* The Christingle originated in Moravia and was introduced into the Anglican church by the Children's Society. These instructions have been produced with the permission of the Children's Society.

The Finger
Spelling
Alphabet

A	B
C	D	E	F	G
H	I	J	K	L
M	N	O	P	Q
R	S	T	U	V
W	X	Y	Z

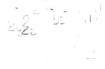